BEATRIX POTTER™
Decoupage

F. WARNE & C⁰

Contents

Contents

Techniques

PREPARING WOODEN SURFACES

Preparing the surfaces of wooden objects, whether old or new, ensures that the finished object is professional-looking and that paint adheres to the wood properly. Using medium grade sandpaper, sand the object to smooth the surface and remove any wax, paint or varnish. Always follow the grain of the wood when sanding or painting. With a damp sponge, wipe any dust off the surface. Finally, thoroughly clean the surface with a sugar soap solution, which will remove any waxy residue.

PREPARING METAL SURFACES

Always treat old metal or enamel surfaces for rust, which will corrode paint and ruin a decoupage item. Rub the item with coarse grade sandpaper to remove any rust, then apply a rust-proofing agent. Finish by painting the object with an oil-based primer. Galvanised metal surfaces are rust-resistant, but should be cleaned before being painted.

PAINTING THE SURFACE

Priming a surface and/or applying an undercoat makes a decoupage object more durable and reduces the likelihood of chipping. Always allow a coat of paint to dry thoroughly before applying the next coat. Objects that will not receive much wear and tear may require only a base coat. Although we have suggested base paint colours for the featured projects, feel free to experiment with different colours, choosing a different paint shade to complement the scraps. The projects in this book call for a variety of paints, including emulsion, acrylic, eggshell and enamel paints, all of which can be obtained at art stores and DIY centres.

Techniques

MIXING A WOODWASH

A woodwash, or woodstain, is a very diluted solution of paint and water which sinks into an unfinished wooden surface. Woodwashes can be purchased ready-made, or can be mixed. To make a woodwash, combine 30% matt emulsion paint with 70% water and mix well. After painting an object with a woodwash, wipe off the excess paint with a cloth, to bring the wood through.

CUTTING OUT SCRAPS

You will find sheets of embossed scraps in the portfolio's right-hand pocket. To cut out these scraps, snip away the connecting strips of paper with sharp manicure scissors. There are additional scraps supplied at the back of this book, on pages 39–48. Remove these pages from the book, then carefully cut out the scraps using a scalpel or craft knife and a cutting mat to protect your work surface. If you wish to make additional scraps, take colour photocopies of the relevant pages before cutting the scraps.

PLANNING YOUR DESIGN

Planning out your decoupage design will help you avoid making disappointing mistakes. First, draw a sketch of how you want your design to look. Using small blobs of reusable adhesive, position your scraps on the object. You may find it easier to use tweezers instead of your fingers when handling small scraps. Aim for a well-balanced, uncluttered design and do not feel limited by the suggested arrangements in this book. When satisfied with your arrangement, remove the scraps one by one.

Techniques

GLUING

PVA glue, also known as white glue, is ideal for decoupage because it dries clear and firmly adheres scraps to almost any surface. Apply PVA glue sparingly to scraps with a fine paintbrush or a glue spreader, available from art shops. Stick the glued scrap on to the surface and smooth out any air bubbles or wrinkles with your finger or a paintbrush. Allow the glue to dry for about 15–20 minutes, then wash the paintbrush or glue spreader when finished.

VARNISHING

Varnishing a decoupage object protects the surface and produces a smooth, shiny finish. Water-based and oil-based varnishes come in a choice of gloss, satin or matt finishes. As a general rule, use a water-based satin or gloss varnish for indoor objects and an oil-based gloss varnish for outdoor objects. Matt varnish is not well-suited to most decoupage, as it becomes cloudy if several coats are applied. It is best to apply varnish by daylight in an environment free of dust and fibres. Ensure that all scraps are firmly stuck down, then paint a thin coat of varnish evenly over the object, using a flip-flopping motion. The number of coats used will depend on the object's purpose. An infrequently handled object, such as a wall clock, will only require one or two coats of varnish. A table, which must be durable, will need many coats of varnish. Water-based varnishes take about two hours to dry, so you can apply four to five coats per day, allowing each coat to dry before applying the next. Oil-based varnishes take longer to dry, ranging from overnight to two weeks. Some projects featured in this book call for cracking varnish. It is important to note that cracking varnish is applied on the top coat of paint to produce cracks, whereas cracking medium is applied between paint layers.

Techniques

FINISHING TOUCHES

The following two techniques should only be used if you have applied at least six coats of varnish, or you will risk damaging the scraps. For a perfectly smooth finish, sand down the penultimate layer of varnish with fine grade sandpaper to remove any visible brush strokes and decrease the paper ridge around the scraps. Sanding keys the surface for a final coat of varnish, enabling you to achieve a smooth, even surface. If you find gloss or satin varnish too shiny for your liking, rub the item down with fine steel wool to key the surface. Massage furniture wax on to the surface with a soft cloth to produce a warm, antiqued appearance.

CLEANING PAINTBRUSHES

After painting, gluing and varnishing, it is important to thoroughly clean your paintbrushes to keep them in good condition. Keep a jar of water near your work surface so you can rinse your brushes immediately. PVA glue, water-based varnishes, emulsion and acrylic paints can be cleaned off with water. Oil-based paints and varnishes can be removed with turpentine or white spirit.

The Study

An ideal way to personalise a
study or office, decoupage can be
used to decorate a variety of
stationery items. Aged for an
old-fashioned effect, Peter Rabbit
magazine files and letter racks look
fun, yet sophisticated, and will keep
the study tidy. As you work, keep
your nearest and dearest close by
in a Peter Rabbit picture frame or
photograph album.

Photograph Album

MATERIALS:

- photograph album
- bookbinding paper
- ruler
- balsa wood
- white woodwash
- soft pencil
- decoupage scraps
- scissors
- PVA glue
- paintbrush
- scalpel and cutting mat
- matt water-based varnish

1. Choose a photograph album that is bound with screws or ribbons. Dismantle the album and measure the cover's dimensions.

2. Copy the album's dimensions on to the back of bookbinding paper in the colour of your choice. Add 2.5 cm (1 inch) to each dimension to allow for a foldover, and cut out the pieces.

3. Cover the front and back of the album with the bookbinding paper. Spread PVA glue thinly and evenly over the back of the paper and smooth it over the album, to prevent air bubbles forming under the paper. Fold the paper's edges over the inside cover, for a neat finish. Reassemble the album.

4. Find an oval-shaped object to use as a template and trace round it on to a piece of balsa wood with a soft pencil.

5. Using a scalpel, carefully cut around the oval shape. Paint the oval with a white woodwash and allow to dry.

6. Print out the word "Photographs" on a computer. Turn the paper over and shade in the back of the type with a soft pencil. Position the type centred, right-side up on the oval. Trace over the letters, which will leave a transfer on the balsa wood. Alternatively, use letter transfers or stencils to write the word. Paint over the letters or leave them as they are, then cover the oval with matt varnish and allow to dry.

7. Cut out your decoupage scraps and position them with the oval panel on the front of the photograph album. Stick the scraps and panel in place with PVA glue. Allow to dry.

Letter Rack

MATERIALS:

- wooden letter rack
- sandpaper
- brown and beige matt emulsion paint
- paintbrushes
- decoupage scraps
- scissors
- reusable adhesive
- PVA glue
- scalpel and cutting mat
- thin balsa wood
- aging varnish
- cracking varnish
- burnt umber oil paint
- paint thinner

1. Sand the letter rack, then paint it with dark brown emulsion paint and allow to dry.

2. Dip just the tip of a dry, coarse brush into the beige emulsion paint. Wipe off any excess paint, then cross-hatch beige sparingly over the brown. Allow the paint to dry.

3. Sand down the corners and edges of the rack with coarse grade sandpaper, allowing the dark brown paint to show through in patches, to create an aged effect.

4. Cut out your decoupage scraps. Stick the large Peter Rabbit scrap on to balsa wood with PVA glue and cut around it with a scalpel. Glue the feet of the raised Peter Rabbit scrap to the inside back of the letter rack, so it sticks up above the rack.

5. Position the other scraps on the letter rack with reusable adhesive. When you are satisfied with the arrangement, remove the scraps one at a time and stick them in place with PVA glue.

6. Paint the letter rack's exterior with aging varnish. After about one and a half hours, paint cracking varnish over the outside of the letter rack, following the instructions on the bottle. The wetter the aging varnish is when the cracking varnish is applied, the larger the cracks will be. To produce small cracks, leave the aging varnish to dry longer, but not for more than three hours. Allow the cracking varnish to dry in a warm place.

7. When the cracking varnish is dry, mix a small amount of burnt umber oil paint with paint thinner. Rub this solution on to the letter rack with a cloth, wiping off the excess liquid with a clean cloth. This solution will emphasise the cracks. Allow to dry.

8. Apply a second coat of aging varnish or a coat of gloss varnish to seal the letter rack.

Magazine Files

MATERIALS:

- wooden magazine file
- sandpaper
- thin balsa wood and scalpel
- decoupage scraps and scissors
- reusable adhesive
- PVA glue
- paintbrush
- matt varnish

FOR THE BLUE FILE:

- 2-inch masking tape
- cornflower white matt emulsion paint
- pale blue woodwash

FOR THE BROWN FILE:

- dark brown and beige matt emulsion paint

BLUE FILE

1.   Sand and prepare the magazine file, then paint it with a blue woodwash. Allow to dry.

2.   Lay strips of masking tape horizontally around the file at equal intervals. Make sure the edges of the tape are level and stuck down well.

3.   Paint between the strips of masking tape with cornflower white matt emulsion paint to create stripes. Take care not to load the paintbrush with too much paint or it will soak under the masking tape.

4.   Once the paint has dried, carefully remove the masking tape by gently pulling it away from the direction of the painted stripe.

5.   Cut out your decoupage scraps, including one large central figure, and arrange them on the magazine file with reusable adhesive. We used the scarecrow from *The Tale of Peter Rabbit* as the central figure, with small birds as details to give additional depth.

6.   Stick the large scrap on to balsa wood with PVA glue and cut it out with a scalpel. Cut out a small square of balsa wood and glue it to the back of the mounted scrap. Glue the raised scrap to the back of the magazine file.

7.   Remove one scrap at a time, peel off the reusable adhesive and stick it in position with PVA glue. Varnish the magazine file with one coat of matt varnish.

BROWN FILE

1.   Sand and finish the magazine file, then paint it with dark brown emulsion paint and allow to dry.

2.   Follow the instructions in steps 2–3 for the letter rack on page 11.

3.   To complete the magazine file, follow steps 5–7 for the blue magazine file, but using Mr. McGregor as the central figure and bees for the details.

Stationery

MATERIALS:

- thin coloured card
- ruler and pencil
- decoupage scraps
- scissors
- PVA glue
- glue spreader

NOTE PAPER

1.   Buy sheets of writing paper or cut a large piece of thin coloured card into sheets the size you desire. There are many types of paper suitable for stationery, such as natural, textured paper or marbled paper. Choose a shade that complements your decoupage scraps.

2.   Cut out a decoupage scrap and stick it on the head of the sheet with a thin coat of PVA glue. You may wish to surround a large

decoupage scrap with several smaller scraps. Decoupage can be used to decorate any type of stationery, from gift tags to greeting cards.

ENVELOPES

1.   Making your own envelopes ensures that they will match and fit your home-made decoupage note paper. Open out an envelope flat to use as a template. Alter the height and width as required, to fit your letter or card.

2.   Choose coloured card in the same shade as your note paper. Copy the envelope's dimensions on the coloured card and cut out this shape. Fold up the bottom and sides of the envelope.

3.   Cut out a decoupage scrap and stick it to the back, triangular flap of the envelope with a thin coat of PVA glue. Allow the glue to dry. When posting the letter, seal the envelope with glue.

The Parlour

Decorated with scraps from
The Tale of Mr. Jeremy Fisher,
this table, vase, picture frame and
clock feature an aquatic theme.
Highlighting decoupage's versatility,
these projects demonstrate how
different finishes can achieve a
period feel. Both homely and
stylish, these furnishings would
look equally appropriate in a formal
parlour or in a casual sitting room.

Flower Vase

MATERIALS:

- clear glass vase with a wide mouth
- turquoise enamel paint
- decoupage scraps
- scissors
- reusable adhesive
- PVA glue
- paintbrush

1. Clean the vase thoroughly to remove any dust and grease. Cut out the fish scraps from pages 46–47.

2. Water down some PVA glue to a creamy consistency. Paint one side of each scrap with this solution and allow them to dry, then paint the opposite sides of the scraps and leave to dry. Repeat this process twice on each side. The PVA glue will prevent paint soaking through the scraps.

3. Position the scraps inside the vase with their coloured sides facing outwards, using small blobs of reusable adhesive to hold them in place.

4. When you are satisfied with your design, remove one scrap at a time and peel off the reusable adhesive. Paint the scrap with the diluted PVA solution, then stick it back in place inside the vase. Repeat this process for every scrap and allow the glue to dry.

5. Paint the inside of the vase with a thin layer of the PVA solution and allow to dry. Using turquoise enamel paint, paint the inside of the vase up to the rim.

6. Allow the paint to dry, then fill the vase with dry or artificial flowers. This vase is not suitable for fresh flowers, as water will cause the paint to run. Water resistant paints are available from most good art stores, but may require firing in a conventional oven.

Wall Clock

MATERIALS:

- wall clock
- medium grade sandpaper
- primer or undercoat
- turquoise enamel paint
- paintbrush
- scissors
- decoupage scraps
- reusable adhesive
- PVA glue

1.   Begin by dismantling the wall clock, making sure to separate the glass, rim, hands and clock face. The glass covering must be detachable from the clock face, or you will not be able to decorate it.

2.   If the clock's rim is wooden, sand it down with medium grade sandpaper and wipe away any dust. Paint the rim with a primer or an undercoat and allow to dry thoroughly.

3.   Paint the rim with turquoise enamel paint and leave it to dry. As enamel paint has a shiny finish, there is no need to varnish the rim.

4.   Cut out your decoupage scraps featuring images from *The Tale of Mr. Jeremy Fisher*. Arrange your scraps around the clock face with reusable adhesive, taking care not to obscure the numbers. When satisfied with the arrangement, peel off the reusable adhesive and stick the scraps into place with a thin coat of PVA glue.

5.   When the paint and glue have dried thoroughly, carefully reassemble the clock and hang it on a wall.

Occasional Table

MATERIALS:

- round, wooden table
- sandpaper
- dark green, turquoise, white and beige matt emulsion paints
- cracking medium
- latex gloves
- decoupage scraps
- reusable adhesive
- scissors
- PVA glue
- paintbrushes
- gloss enamel varnish

1.   Begin by sanding the table, as explained on page 4 in the techniques section, to remove any paint, wax or varnish. When the table is prepared, paint the top and bottom of the table with dark green matt emulsion paint. Use a coarse paintbrush to produce visible brushwork. Allow the paint to dry.

2.   Cross-hatch cracking medium over the tabletop and allow it to dry thoroughly. Vary the direction of your brush strokes, or the cracks will not look natural.

3.   Water down a small amount of turquoise matt emulsion paint to a milky consistency. Paint this over the cracking medium on the tabletop and allow to dry. Cracks will begin to form, revealing the green paint underneath.

4.   Using fine sandpaper, lightly rub over the tabletop to smooth out any rough areas. Age the table by sanding around the edges to expose small areas of wood and green paint.

5.   Mix equal portions of white and beige matt emulsion paints. Dilute this mixture to a very thin consistency, 80% water to 20% paint. Liberally brush this solution over the table top and bottom, following the grain of the wood.

6.   Wearing latex gloves, rub the paint into the surface of the table top to produce a clear, watery effect. Allow the paint to dry.

7.   Using medium grade sandpaper, rub away small areas of paint on the table's legs, replicating normal wear and tear by allowing small patches of wood to show through.

8.   Cut out your decoupage scraps and arrange them on the tabletop using reusable adhesive. We positioned Jeremy Fisher scraps around one side of the table with fish and marine life around the opposite side. Once satisfied with the placement of the scraps, stick them in position with a thin coat of PVA glue.

9.   When the glue has dried, liberally cover the entire table, top and legs, with a coat of gloss enamel varnish. Give the tabletop five to six coats of varnish, allowing the varnish to dry between coats.

Picture Frame

MATERIALS:

- wide-rimmed, wooden picture frame
- medium grade sandpaper
- dark green emulsion paint
- thin balsa wood
- PVA glue
- decoupage scraps
- scissors
- scalpel and cutting mat
- paintbrushes
- gloss enamel varnish

1.   Sand down the picture frame and prepare the surface as explained on page 4. Paint the front and back of the frame with one coat of green emulsion paint. Allow the paint to dry thoroughly.

2.   Using medium grade sandpaper, sand away sections of the paint, particularly at the frame's joints and edges, to produce an aged effect. Wipe away the dust with a damp cloth.

3.   Cut out the large Jeremy Fisher scraps and stick them on to balsa wood with PVA glue. Carefully cut around the scraps with a scalpel.

4.   Cut out two small squares of balsa wood and stick one to the back of each mounted scrap. These raised scraps will give the frame a three-dimensional effect.

5.   Glue the large, raised scraps on the bottom edge of the frame. Cut out the smaller decoupage scraps and stick them around the frame. Allow the glue to dry, then cover the frame, front and back, with a coat of varnish.

The picture frame depicted on page 8 was made following this method, but using dark blue paint and a Peter Rabbit motif.

The Boudoir

This elegant decoupage dressing table ensemble will enhance the bedroom of any Beatrix Potter fan, young or old. Favourite Peter Rabbit scenes add a hint of playfulness to a graceful brush and comb set with matching mirrors. Distressed for an antique feel, a decoupage jewellery box makes a perfect cache for precious heirlooms or mementos.

Lampshade

MATERIALS:

FOR BOTH LAMPSHADES
- heat-proof, blue canvas lampshade
- decoupage scraps
- scissors
- reusable adhesive
- PVA glue
- paintbrush
- gloss water-based varnish

FOR LAMPSHADE 2
- tailor's chalk or fabric pen
- bookbinding paper

LAMPSHADE 1

1.   Remove the lampshade from the lamp. Cut out enough running rabbit decoupage scraps to fit around the circumference of the lampshade. Position the scraps around the lampshade at equal intervals with reusable adhesive.

2.   When satisfied with the design, remove the scraps one by one, peel off the reusable adhesive and stick the scraps in place with PVA glue. Varnish the lampshade and allow to dry.

LAMPSHADE 2

1.   Remove the lampshade from the lamp. Cut out enough running rabbit scraps to fit halfway around the lampshade. Cut out seedling decoupage scraps, as well.

2.   Place one of the rabbit scraps right-side down on the bookbinding paper. Trace around the scrap with tailor's chalk and cut it out. Cut out the same number of silhouettes as you have running rabbit scraps.

3.   Position the scraps and silhouettes alternately around the lampshade, then stick them in place with PVA glue. Glue the seedlings at equal intervals around the base of the lampshade, between the rabbits.

Jewellery Box

MATERIALS:

- small wooden chest
- fine grade sandpaper
- dark blue and white emulsion paint
- paintbrushes
- decoupage scraps
- scissors
- reusable adhesive
- PVA glue
- gold marker pen
- aging varnish
- cracking varnish
- paint thinner
- white oil paint
- gloss varnish

1.   Dismantle the jewellery box, removing the hinges and clasp. Sand and prepare the wooden surfaces, as explained on page 4.

2.   Paint the jewellery box's interior and exterior with dark blue emulsion paint. Use a coarse paintbrush to produce visible brushwork rather than a smooth finish. Allow paint to dry.

3.   Water down a small quantity of white emulsion paint to make a woodwash with a runny consistency. Paint the woodwash over the exterior of the box and allow to dry.

4.   Age the jewellery box by gently rubbing down the edges with fine grade sandpaper. This will expose small areas of wood and give the box the appearance of natural wear.

5.   Cut out your decoupage scraps and position them on the box with reusable adhesive. When satisfied with the arrangement, remove the scraps one at a time and stick them in place with PVA glue. Allow the glue to dry.

6.   Using a gold marker pen, draw freehand flourishes on the top of the box, between the scraps. When the ink has dried, paint the outside of the box with aging varnish.

7.   After about one and a half to two hours, paint the exterior of the box with cracking varnish and allow to dry thoroughly.

8.   Mix a small amount of paint thinner with a small quantity of white oil paint. Rub this solution on the cracked varnish all over the box with a cloth. Wipe off the excess liquid with a kitchen towel. The oil paint will fill in the crac ing them visible. Allow to dry.

9.   Paint the box with a coat of gloss, water-based varnish and allow to dry. Reassemble the jewellery box, replacing the fixtures.

Vanity Set

MATERIALS:

- wooden brush, comb and mirror
- sandpaper
- masking tape
- primer and undercoat
- dark blue eggshell paint
- decoupage scraps
- scissors
- reusable adhesive
- PVA glue
- paintbrushes
- pencil
- gold marker pen
- gloss varnish

1. Clean and sand the wooden comb, brush and hand-held mirror set. Lay strips of masking tape along the edges of the mirror and around the bristles of the brush, to keep them clean.

2. Paint the wooden items with a coat of primer. When the primer has dried, paint them with undercoat and allow to dry.

3. Paint the wood with a coat of dark blue eggshell paint and allow to dry thoroughly.

4. Cut out your decoupage scraps and position them with small blobs of reusable adhesive along the handles and backs of the mirror, comb and brush. On each object we used one large central scrap and several smaller details. You may find it easier to position very small scraps using tweezers. When you are happy with the arrangement, remove the scraps one at a time, take off the reusable adhesive and stick the scraps down with PVA glue.

5. When the glue has dried, lightly draw curly, freehand flourishes in pencil between the decoupage scraps on the handles and around the central figures. Carefully trace over the pencil lines with a gold marker pen.

6. When the marker pen has dried, carefully rub off any visible pencil marks. Paint the handles and backs with three or more coats of gloss varnish, allowing each coat to dry thoroughly before applying the next one. Remove the masking tape when dry.

Dressing Table Mirror

MATERIALS:

- freestanding wooden mirror
- sandpaper
- masking tape
- primer
- undercoat
- dark blue eggshell paint
- decoupage scraps
- scissors
- reusable adhesive
- PVA glue
- paintbrushes
- pencil
- gold marker pen
- gloss varnish

1. Clean and sand the mirror. Lay strips of masking tape along the edges of the mirror, to keep the glass clean.

2. Paint the mirror frame with a coat of primer. When the primer has dried, paint the mirror frame with undercoat and allow to dry.

3. Paint the mirror frame with a coat of dark blue eggshell paint and allow it to dry.

4. Cut out your decoupage scraps and position them around the mirror frame with reusable adhesive, leaving spaces between each paper cutout. When you are happy with the arrangement, remove the scraps one at a time, peel off the reusable adhesive and stick them in place with PVA glue.

5. Using a pencil, lightly draw curly, freehand twiddles between the decoupage scraps around the frame. Carefully trace over the pencil lines with a fine-tipped gold marker pen.

6. When the marker pen has dried, gingerly rub off any visible pencil marks. Paint the frame with approximately three coats of varnish, allowing each coat to dry completely before applying the next one. Remove the masking tape when the varnish is dry.

The Nursery

The adventures of Peter Rabbit
and his friends have been beloved
by children for over a century.
What better theme for decorating
your child's nursery than the
delightful Tales of Beatrix Potter?
Decoupage furnishings, such as a
chair for reading bedtime stories or
an upholstered toy chest for storing
favourite games, transform a
modern playroom into a
traditional nursery.

Child's Chair

MATERIALS:

- unfinished wooden chair
- sandpaper
- white and red matt emulsion paint
- pencil
- decoupage scraps
- scissors
- reusable adhesive
- PVA glue
- paintbrushes
- blue wax colouring pencil
- black permanent marker pen
- yellow marker pen
- matt varnish

1.   Prepare the surface of an unfinished wooden chair, as explained on page 4. Mix 40% white paint with 60% water and brush this solution liberally over the chair. Wipe away the excess with a paper towel, to bring the wood through, and allow to dry.

2.   Using a pencil, lightly draw a freehand square on the seat of the chair. Draw a rough tartan design inside the square, then draw freehand flourishes and twiddles along the back and legs of the chair. If you make a mistake, simply erase the lines and start again.

3.   Draw a wavy line around the tartan square on the chair's seat. Fill in this border with undiluted white emulsion paint, to simulate lace trimming. Allow the paint to dry.

4.   Draw over the tartan design with red paint. Try varying the thickness of the lines and watering down the red paint to create different tones. When the paint is dry, define the edges of the white "lace" border with a thin, permanent black marker pen. Use the marker to draw tassels on each corner of the seat and fill them in with a yellow marker pen. Draw over the pencil twiddles with a sharp, blue wax pencil.

5.   Cut out your scraps and position them on the chair's legs and back with reusable adhesive. Choose small scraps for the legs. When satisfied with the design, remove the scraps one by one, peel off the adhesive and stick them in place with PVA glue. Apply a coat of matt varnish when the glue is dry.

Money Box

MATERIALS:

- empty container with a plastic lid
- ruler
- emulsion paint or thick coloured paper
- paintbrush
- decoupage scraps
- reusable adhesive
- PVA glue
- scissors
- scalpel
- cutting mat
- permanent marker pen
- satin acrylic varnish

1.   Measure the height of the container and cut out a rectangle of coloured paper to fit around it, allowing for a 2.5 cm (1 inch) overlap. Stick the paper around the container with PVA glue, making sure to spread the glue evenly to avoid air bubbles. Alternatively, paint the container with emulsion paint in the colour of your choice and allow to dry. A miniature paint sample, available from DIY centres, would be ideal, as only a small amount is required.

2.   Cut out your decoupage scraps and position them around the container, using reusable adhesive to hold them in place.

3.   When satisfied with your arrangement, stick the scraps down with a thin coat of PVA glue and leave to dry. Apply a coat of satin acrylic varnish and allow to dry.

4.   Place the container's plastic lid flat on a cutting mat. Using a permanent marker pen, draw an oblong shape on the lid, to serve as a money slot. Carefully cut out the slot using a scalpel. If the lid has a date printed on it, remove the print by rubbing it gently with steel wool.

5.   Cut out a small decoupage scrap, such as a butterfly or a bee, to decorate the lid. Stick the scrap on to the lid with PVA glue. There is no need to varnish the lid.

Toy Chest

MATERIALS:

- wooden toy chest
- cornflower white matt emulsion paint
- blue woodwash
- decoupage scraps
- scissors
- reusable adhesive
- PVA glue
- matt varnish
- paintbrushes
- wadding
- green velvet
- upholstery tacks
- upholstery ribbon
- staple gun

1. Sand the wooden toy chest and prepare the wood as described on page 4. If the toy chest's lid is hinged, remove the hinges. Paint a border around each side of the chest using a blue woodwash. Allow the paint to dry.

2. Paint inside the blue borders on each side of the chest with cornflower white matt emulsion paint and allow to dry.

3. Cut out your large decoupage scraps and arrange them around the toy chest with reusable adhesive. When satisfied with the arrangement, remove the scraps one by one, peel off the reusable adhesive and glue them in place with PVA glue. Allow the glue to dry.

4. Paint over all four sides of the toy chest with matt varnish and allow to dry.

5. Cut a piece of wadding to fit the measurement of the chest's lid. Continue adding layers of the same dimensions until you are satisfied with the amount of cushioning.

6. Cut a piece of green velvet to fit the measurement of the lid, adding 25 cm (10 inches) to all four sides.

7. Place the wadding on top of the lid and lay the fabric on top of the wadding. To ensure that the wadding stays in place and does not spill over the edges of the lid, staple the wadding to the lid with a staple gun.

8. Turn the lid upside down. Fold the fabric tightly underneath one of the long edges and staple it in place with a staple gun. Repeat this process for the second long edge and then each of the short edges. Trim off any excess fabric on the underside of the lid. Apply PVA glue along each raw edge of the velvet to stop it fraying, then glue upholstery ribbon along the seam to seal the fabric.

9. Press upholstery tacks along the outside edge of the lid for added sturdiness and an attractive finish. Replace the hinges on the lid if necessary.

Storage Box

MATERIALS:

- self-assembly cardboard storage box
- ruler
- wrapping paper
- scissors
- spray glue adhesive
- decoupage scraps
- reusable adhesive
- PVA glue
- glue spreader
- spray acrylic varnish

1.   While the box is collapsed, measure the dimensions of each side and note them down.

2.   Copy out the box's dimensions on to the back of solid-coloured wrapping paper, adding 1 cm (½ inch) to the length and width to allow for folded edges.

3.   Cut out the pieces of wrapping paper and stick them to the cardboard pieces using spray glue adhesive. Fold the edges of the paper over for a neat finish. If the box has a lid, repeat steps 1–3. Assemble the box.

4.   Cut out your decoupage scraps, then position them on the box and lid with reusable adhesive. We have achieved a bold, graphic look using one large scrap on each side of the box.

5.   When satisfied with your design, remove the scraps one at a time, peel off the reusable adhesive and stick them in place with PVA glue. Allow the glue to dry.

6.   If the box requires added durability, you can spray it with acrylic varnish. Do not use liquid varnish, as it will warp the box.

The Garden

*Peter Rabbit, that incorrigible
nibbler of Mr. McGregor's radishes
and lettuces, makes a winsome
motif for garden accessories.
Quaint touches, such as a Peter
Rabbit garden sign, imbue even the
smallest urban garden with classic,
countryside charm. Practical as well
as attractive, these decoupage
objects are durable enough to
withstand outdoor use.*

Bird House

MATERIALS:

- wooden bird house
- sandpaper
- primer
- undercoat
- pale green and dark green eggshell paint
- paintbrush
- decoupage scraps
- scissors
- reusable adhesive
- PVA glue
- oil-based gloss varnish

1.   Sand the bird house and prepare the surfaces, as described on page 4. After wiping off any dust, paint the bird house with a coat of primer and allow to dry.

2.   Paint the bird house with undercoat and allow to dry. As the bird house is intended for outdoor use, it requires more coats of paint and varnish than indoor furnishings.

3.   Cover the main body of the bird house with a coat of pale green eggshell paint, then paint the roof with dark green eggshell paint and leave to dry. If you prefer, paint the bird house with pale blue and dark blue paints instead.

4.   Position your decoupage scraps around the bird house with reusable adhesive. When satisfied with the arrangement, remove the scraps one at a time, peel off the adhesive and stick them in place using PVA glue.

5.   When the glue has dried, paint the bird house with at least four coats of oil-based gloss varnish, allowing each coat to dry thoroughly before applying the next. Now the bird house is ready to be hung outdoors.

Seed Markers

MATERIALS:

- piece of wood,
3 cm. wide, 5 mm thick
(1¼ inches wide, ¼ inch thick)
- hand saw
- sandpaper
- white woodstain
- paintbrush
- decoupage scraps
- scissors
- PVA glue
- oil-based gloss varnish
- white sticky labels
- water-proof marker pen

1.   Cut the strip of wood into 20 cm (8 inch) lengths using a small hand saw. Saw a point at one end of each piece, so the seed markers can be stuck into the soil.

2.   Sand down the edges of each marker, to smooth any snags in the wood. Wipe away the dust with a damp cloth.

3.   Paint each marker on both sides with a coat of white woodstain. If you prefer, you can paint the markers a colour or leave them plain. Allow the woodstain to dry overnight.

4.   Position a decoupage scrap on the unpointed end of each marker and stick it in place with PVA glue. Allow the glue to dry.

5.   Varnish both sides of each marker at least four times, allowing each coat to dry before applying the next.

6.   Write the names of the seeds you are planting on white labels using a water-proof marker pen. Stick the labels on the markers, then position the seed markers in your garden.

Garden Signs

WORKING IN THE GARDEN

1. Sand the surfaces and edges of a rectangular piece of wood until smooth.

2. Paint the entire sign with white woodstain and allow to dry.

3. Cut out the decoupage scraps. Plan your design on paper first, to ensure that the scraps and lettering will fit on the sign. When satisfied with the arrangement, stick your decoupage scraps on the wood with PVA glue. Add the type to the sign, using either stencils, printed type or transfers. Draw a light pencil guideline with a ruler, so the type will be straight.

4. Varnish the sign with an oil-based gloss varnish. As the sign is for outdoor use, apply at least four coats of varnish, allowing each coat to dry before adding the next.

5. Insert two eye screws at opposite ends of one long edge of the wooden rectangle. Thread a length of garden twine through the two eye screws and twist off the ends securely. Hang the sign outdoors on the garden gate.

PETER RABBIT'S GARDEN SIGN

1. Using a hand saw, cut one end of the narrow piece of wood into a point, so the sign can be stuck into the ground. If you wish, cut a curve along the length of the other piece of wood using a jigsaw. Sand the surfaces and edges of both pieces until smooth and even.

MATERIALS:

- hand saw
- sandpaper
- white woodstain
- paintbrushes
- decoupage scraps and scissors
- PVA glue
- stencils and marker pen, transfers, or printed type
- pencil and ruler
- oil-based gloss varnish

FOR "WORKING IN THE GARDEN":
- piece of wood, 30 x 60 cm (12 x 24 inches), 9 mm (½ inch) thick
- 2 eye screws
- garden twine

FOR "PETER RABBIT'S GARDEN":
- piece of wood, 30 x 65 cm (12 x 26 inches), 9 mm (½ inch) thick
- piece of wood: 30 x 2 cm (12 x 1 inch), 9 mm (½ inch) thick
- 2 screws
- drill

2. Drill two holes in the non-pointed end of the narrow piece of wood. Position this end in the centre of the larger piece. Insert screws in the holes and tighten to attach the two pieces.

3. Now follow the instructions in steps 2–4 for the "Working in the garden" sign.

Watering Can

MATERIALS:

- galvanised watering can
- green enamel spray paint
- pale green enamel paint
  - decoupage scraps
    - scissors
  - reusable adhesive
    - pencil
    - PVA glue
- fine black permanent water-proof marker pen
  - paintbrushes
- water-based varnish
- oil-based gloss varnish

1.   Clean and dry the watering can. Cover your work surface with newspaper and spray the can's exterior with green enamel paint. You may need to use several coats to achieve an even finish. Allow the paint to dry.

2.   Cut out your rabbit decoupage scraps and arrange them around the watering can with reusable adhesive, leaving generous gaps between the scraps.

3.   Using a soft pencil, draw freehand seedlings in the spaces between the scraps.

4.   Remove the scraps one by one. Peel off the reusable adhesive and stick the scraps firmly back into position with PVA glue.

5.   Fill in the seedling outlines with pale green enamel paint and a fine paintbrush. When the paint has dried, carefully outline around the seedlings with a permanent black marker pen and leave to dry overnight.

6.   Seal the watering can with a water-based varnish and leave to dry. Apply at least four coats of a hard-wearing, oil-based gloss varnish, allowing each coat to dry before adding the next. The more coats of varnish you use, the more durable the watering can will be.

FREDERICK WARNE
Published by the Penguin Group
Penguin Books Ltd, 27 Wrights Lane, London W8 5TZ, England
Penguin Putnam Inc., 375 Hudson Street, New York, NY 10014, USA
Penguin Books Australia Ltd, Ringwood, Victoria, Australia
Penguin Books Canada Ltd, 10 Alcorn Avenue, Toronto, Ontario, Canada M4V 3B2
Penguin Books (N.Z.) Ltd, 182-190 Wairau Road, Auckland 10, New Zealand

Penguin Books Ltd, Registered Offices: Harmondsworth, Middlesex, England

Please visit our web site: www.peterrabbit.com

First published 1999 by Frederick Warne
1 3 5 7 9 10 8 6 4 2

ISBN 0 7232 4445 6

Photography by Tim Hill
Styling by Zoë Hill
Projects devised and created by Eliz Hüseyin
Decoupage scraps supplied courtesy of Mamelok Press Ltd, Bury St Edmunds

Colour reproduction by Saxon Photolitho Ltd, Norwich
Manufactured in China by Imago Publishing Ltd

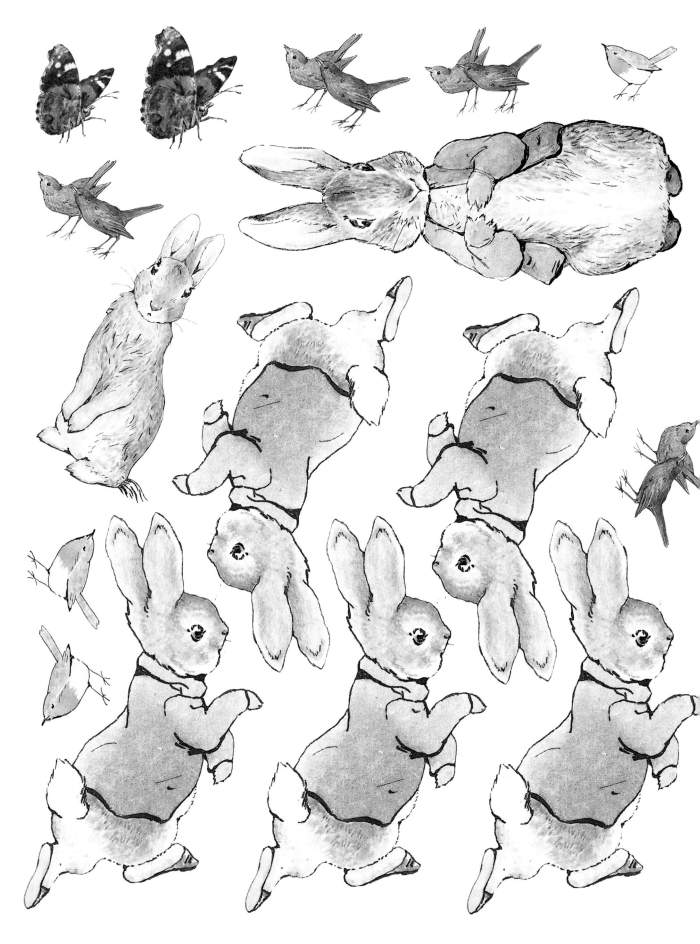